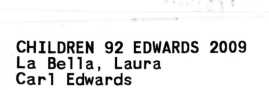

Behind The Wheel™

Carl Edwards

NASCAR Driver

Laura La Bella

rosen publishing's
rosen central®

New York

*For my father, a dedicated NASCAR fan
and an all-around "car guy"*

Published in 2009 by The Rosen Publishing Group, Inc.
29 East 21st Street, New York, NY 10010

Library of Congress Cataloging-in-Publication Data

La Bella, Laura.
Carl Edwards: NASCAR driver / Laura La Bella.—1st ed.
        p. cm.—(Behind the wheel)
Includes bibliographical references and index.
ISBN-13: 978-1-4042-1898-7 (library binding)
ISBN-13: 978-1-4358-5405-5 (pbk)
ISBN-13: 978-1-4358-5411-6 (6 pack)
1. Edwards, Carl, 1979– 2. Stock car drivers—United States—Biography.
I. Title.
GV1032.E39L3 2009
796.72092—dc22
[B]

2008022087

Manufactured in the United States of America

On the cover: Carl Edwards, driver of the #99 Rousch Racing Home
Depot Ford, sits in his car during practice for the NASCAR Nextel
Cup MBNA RacePoints 400 at Dover International Speedway in
Dover, Delaware.

CONTENTS

Introduction 4

Chapter ① Born to Race 6

Chapter ② Building a Career 14

Chapter ③ Troubles and Triumphs 23

Chapter ④ Off the Track 32

Glossary 42

For More Information 44

For Further Reading 45

Bibliography 46

Index 47

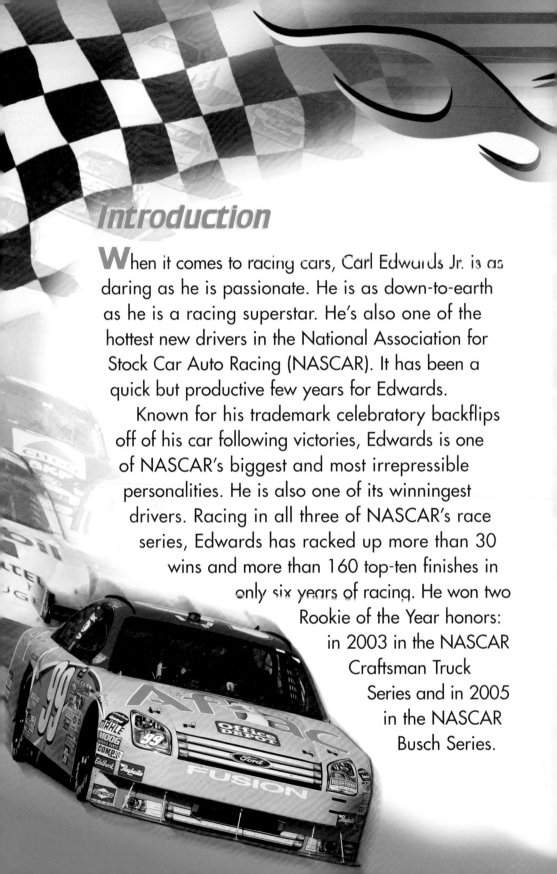

Introduction

When it comes to racing cars, Carl Edwards Jr. is as daring as he is passionate. He is as down-to-earth as he is a racing superstar. He's also one of the hottest new drivers in the National Association for Stock Car Auto Racing (NASCAR). It has been a quick but productive few years for Edwards.

Known for his trademark celebratory backflips off of his car following victories, Edwards is one of NASCAR's biggest and most irrepressible personalities. He is also one of its winningest drivers. Racing in all three of NASCAR's race series, Edwards has racked up more than 30 wins and more than 160 top-ten finishes in only six years of racing. He won two Rookie of the Year honors: in 2003 in the NASCAR Craftsman Truck Series and in 2005 in the NASCAR Busch Series.

With a signature backflip, NASCAR driver Carl Edwards shows off why he's at the top of his game. The driver has garnered worldwide attention for winning more than 30 races.

In 2007, Edwards was named the NASCAR Busch Series champion.

Not yet 30 years old, Edwards should have a long and successful future ahead of him in racing. His life story is far from written, but what an adventure it has already been!

CHAPTER 1

Born to Race

Carl Edwards Jr. was born on August 15, 1979, in Columbia, Missouri. Almost his whole life has been about racing cars. His father, Carl Edwards Sr., raced modified stock cars and midget sprint cars for more than 40 years. Edwards was also close with his uncle, Bill Schrader, and spent considerable time with his cousin, Ken Schrader, a Nextel Cup driver. Discovering an interest in cars, Edwards began building and racing Volkswagen race cars. He raced locally in Missouri and Illinois, then began racing in several other states throughout the Midwest. Edwards has competed in more than 400 races throughout his career as a driver.

Growing Up at the Track

Carl and his younger brother, Kenny, who currently

drives in NASCAR's Hornet Division, grew up at the tracks where their father raced. Their mother, Nancy Sterling, would bring them to their father's races, where they would watch him drive and help out in the pits. Carl remembers hanging out at racetracks with his father and brother.

For Edwards, racing is a family affair. He and his brother grew up watching their father, Carl Sr., race.

When Carl was too young to race, he and his brother played while their father competed.

As he got older, he began to experience a different side of the life at a track. He told reporter Nikki Krone that "I started going with Dad into the pits and helping out a little bit. I just remember being at the races in Pevely, Missouri, and being at the fence and watching Dad hot-lap it. I remember the day real well because I could see his hands real well in the car. The sun was still out, and the track was pretty dry. I remember watching him and hearing the car. I thought, man, I could do that. So I started bugging Dad, you know, like every racer who has bugged his parents."

Soon, Carl was learning about auto racing firsthand. He helped his father in the pit, worked on the cars, and finally got a chance to have his first driving experience. At the age of 14, he started hot lapping his dad's car. Hot lapping is driving around a racetrack without competing for a position. Even though it is not the same as competitive racing, drivers' times are often recorded to determine whether their driving performance is improving. "I'd kind of hang out in the truck until right before hot laps started," Carl says. "And then [my dad would] sign in as the driver, and we'd be in the back of the pit area. Nobody would really notice, and I'd just kind of slip in the car and go race" (as quoted by Krone).

A First Taste of Victory and Hard Work

Edwards Sr. was the first to see the natural talent his son had behind the wheel. Impressed by his son's driving while hot lapping, he started signing him up for races in 1993, when Carl was only 13 years old. He started racing four-cylinder mini-sprints, which are small cars powered by a motorcycle engine. In 1994, Carl won four feature races in the mini-sprint series at tracks in Missouri and Illinois.

Supporting his son's enthusiasm behind the wheel, Edwards Sr. bought a car, fixed it up, and began bringing Carl to different tracks each week. In just three short years, Carl had a total of 14 wins in the 1994, 1995, and 1996 mini-sprint race seasons. But Edwards Sr. expected his son to do more than just learn to drive. "When [Carl] decided he wanted to race, I kind of made him work for it," he told reporter Nikki Krone. "He had to come over and work on both cars as much as he was able, and he learned quite a bit as far as getting the cars ready to go racing and all that stuff. He'd come over and charge batteries, air up tires, change oil, and help do engine tuning and whatever had to be done. He'd ice down the cooler and get everything ready to go, because that was part of the deal. But he really liked racing, so he worked pretty hard to do it."

When Edwards expressed an interest in racing, his father encouraged him to start out racing four-cylinder mini-sprints.

At the time, Carl wanted to focus on developing his driving skills and wasn't nearly as interested in working on the cars themselves. He later told FrontStretch.com, an online NASCAR magazine, that, despite his lack of interest and enthusiasm, working on the cars turned out to be a great learning experience that actually made him a better race car driver. "I think [my dad] liked having me race with him because I did all the maintenance on both cars when we raced," Carl said in the interview with FrontStretch.com. "I wanted to race so bad that it didn't really matter. It was kind of a different situation than I envisioned when we started racing together. I figured he'd be right there showing me how to do everything and helping me out. As it turned out, it actually was better for me that I did virtually all the work on my own as soon as I could. When I first started, he obviously was doing a lot more work, but as soon as I could do something on my own, he wouldn't help me on it anymore. It was frustrating at first, but I could always go to him, and he would explain things to me. In the end, I'm really grateful that I did so much without any help."

The experience also strengthened Carl's relationship with his father. "We butted heads in just about every other aspect of life, and the neat thing about racing was we got along perfectly," Carl said in the interview with FrontStretch.com. "We had great communication. It was unbelievable how well we got along at the racetrack."

A Growing Need for Speed

At the age of 16, Carl went to Charlotte, North Carolina, to spend the summer with his cousin, Ken Schrader, who is still a fixture in NASCAR. Schrader had a solid career in racing. He was named the 1980 USAC Stock Car Rookie of the Year, the 1982 USAC Silver Crown Champion, the

Growing up, Edwards began spending time with his cousin, NASCAR driver Ken Schrader *(left)*, who drove for the Hendrick Racing Team during the 1991 season.

1983 USAC Sprint Car Champion, and the 1985 NASCAR Rookie of the Year.

Carl helped out in Schrader's race shop and watched his cousin compete in races. At the end of the summer, Carl returned to Missouri. He was now more determined than ever to become a race car driver. Before he left North Carolina, Schrader gave Carl some advice. He told his young cousin to start gaining experience on dirt tracks driving a modified car, which is a vehicle that has been upgraded with parts and other components to enhance its performance. Carl purchased a car and began driving in the IMCA modified races. The IMCA, or International Motor Contest Association, was organized in 1915. It is currently the oldest active auto racing sanctioning body in the United States.

Carl began driving in IMCA races in 1998 and immediately did well. That first year, he won the Rookie of the Year award in the IMCA modified division. Over the next two years, he honed his racing skills. He won two track championships at Capital Speedway in Holts Summit, Missouri, in 1999 and 2000. He then competed in two more racing series, the Baby Grand Division and the USAC Silver Crown Series, both in 2001.

While he continued to race, Carl enrolled at the University of Missouri and worked as a substitute teacher. But while he was a natural with children in the classroom, his real passion continued to be driving, so he soon set his sights on the pinnacle of racing achievement. Carl Edwards set out to become a NASCAR driver.

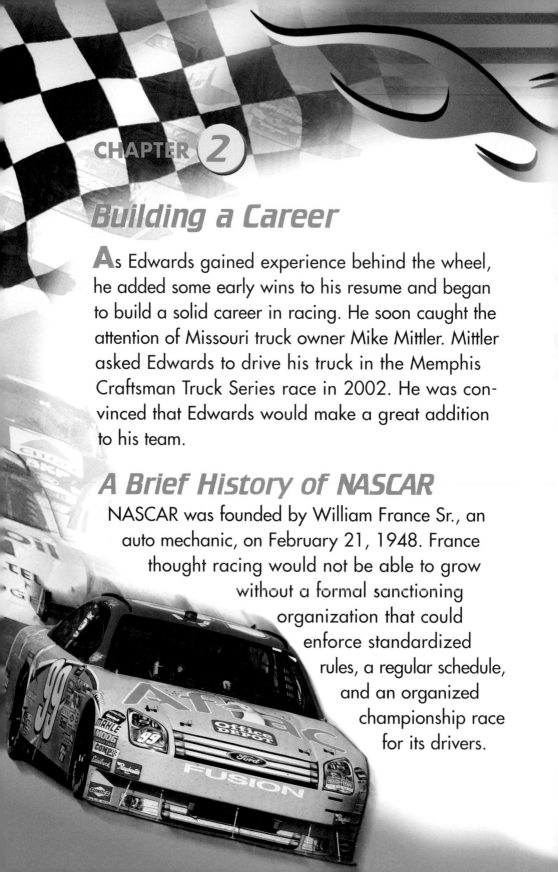

CHAPTER 2

Building a Career

As Edwards gained experience behind the wheel, he added some early wins to his resume and began to build a solid career in racing. He soon caught the attention of Missouri truck owner Mike Mittler. Mittler asked Edwards to drive his truck in the Memphis Craftsman Truck Series race in 2002. He was convinced that Edwards would make a great addition to his team.

A Brief History of NASCAR

NASCAR was founded by William France Sr., an auto mechanic, on February 21, 1948. France thought racing would not be able to grow without a formal sanctioning organization that could enforce standardized rules, a regular schedule, and an organized championship race for its drivers.

When NASCAR was just beginning, the Daytona International Speedway was an old dirt track where drivers drove around a barrier of crashed cars that lined the outside of the track.

NASCAR hosted its first event at a racetrack in Daytona Beach, Florida. In the post-war years, NASCAR grew slowly but steadily as people started to learn more about stock car racing.

Today, NASCAR is the largest sanctioning body of motor sports in the United States. The three largest racing series overseen by NASCAR are the Sprint Cup Series (formerly known as the Winston Cup and the Nextel Cup Series), the Nationwide Series (formerly known as the

15

Busch Series), and the Craftsman Truck Series. The Sprint Cup Series features stock cars, as does the Nationwide Series, which has a shorter season and less prize money than the Sprint Cup Series. The Craftsman Truck Series features modified racing pickup trucks. In addition, NASCAR also oversees more than 1,200 races at 100 tracks in 30 U.S. states, in Canada, and in Mexico. The organization is based in Daytona Beach, Florida, but also has offices in North Carolina, New York, Los Angeles, Mexico City, and Toronto, Canada.

NASCAR has grown to become the number one spectator sport in the United States and the top-rated motor sport on Canadian television. It is the number two-rated regular season sport on American television, ranking only behind the National Football League (NFL). NASCAR races are broadcast in more than 150 countries and in more than 30 languages. NASCAR's drivers are known around the world. So, it's no surprise that Carl Edwards would jump at the chance to drive for one of the highest-profile racing teams in NASCAR, the highest-profile racing organization in the world.

Edwards's Early NASCAR Years

During the 2002 season, Edwards competed in seven truck races for MB Motorsports, Mittler's team. As he was getting ready to compete in more races for Mittler in the

Edwards's wins have been enough to set him apart in NASCAR, but fans have gravitated toward his showmanship. Edwards celebrates each win with a crowd-pleasing backflip.

2003 season, however, he received a phone call that changed his life and put him on a path toward an even brighter future in racing.

On the other end of the phone was Jack Roush, owner of Roush Fenway Racing. The Roush Fenway team included some of the best drivers in NASCAR, including Mark Martin, who won 35 NASCAR races and finished second place in the overall point standings four times. Impressed with Edwards's driving ability, Roush Fenway sought out the young driver to see if he'd be interested in driving the #99 Ford F-150 truck for the Roush Racing team. Edwards jumped at the chance to drive for one of NASCAR's premier teams.

During his first season with Roush Fenway, Edwards quickly impressed his new team. Edwards, in a #99 Ford truck sponsored by Superchips and Charter Communications, competed in 25 races during the 2003 season. He earned one pole position, three wins, 13 top-five finishes, and 15 top-ten finishes. His success earned him the Raybestos Rookie of the Year title and an eighth place finish in the final point standings.

Edwards also kicked off the 2004 NASCAR Craftsman Truck season with a big win. He won the season-opener at the Daytona International Speedway, which is home to the famous Daytona 500 car race. He followed up that victory with a win at the Kansas Speedway in July and then captured a third win at the Bristol Motor Speedway.

Making the Leap to Stock Cars and the Cup Series

In August 2004, Jack Roush gave Edwards the chance of a lifetime: he moved the young driver up to the Nextel Cup Series, now called the Sprint Cup Series. The Sprint Cup Series is NASCAR's top racing series.

Edwards was now driving the #99 Roush Fenway Racing Ford Taurus. He began to race in the Sprint

Series while he continued to compete on the Craftsman Truck schedule. (Many NASCAR drivers compete in all three of the main NASCAR series simultaneously, racing trucks one day and stock cars the next.) Edwards made his debut in the Sprint Cup Series at the Michigan International Speedway, where he brought home a tenth place finish—a significant accomplishment for the young driver. Edwards, along with just four other drivers—Matt Kenseth (his teammate at Roush Fenway), Rusty Wallace, Terry Labonte, and Kyle Petty—are the only five active Sprint Cup drivers to finish inside the top ten in their first career Cup starts.

Edwards ended the year with an outstanding showing. He went on to finish fourth in the overall Craftsman Truck Series standings, while he finished the Sprint Cup Series with five top-ten finishes. His best was a third place finish at the Atlanta Motor Speedway.

In 2005, Edwards left the Craftsman Truck Series to focus exclusively on stock car racing. He took on both the Sprint Cup and the Busch Cup Series full time. The Busch Series, now called the Nationwide Series, sponsors stock car races that are held the day before the Sprint Series races, at the same tracks. The Nationwide Series is a proving ground for drivers looking to excel in the Sprint Series. Edwards did extremely well in both series. The highlight of the season for Edwards was on March 19, 2005, when he won the Aaron's 312 at the Atlanta

In the same March weekend in 2005, at the Atlanta Motor Speedway, Edwards became the first driver in NASCAR history to win two races back to back in the same weekend.

Motor Speedway. This was his first Busch Series win. The next day, on the same track, he beat driver Jimmie Johnson by a mere 200ths of a second to win the Golden Corral 500 for his first Nextel Cup Series win. Until this took place, no driver had ever won both the Busch and Nextel Cup Series races in the same weekend at Atlanta.

As he had the year before in the Craftsman Truck Series, Edwards was awarded Raybestos Rookie of the

NASCAR GRABS THE NATION'S ATTENTION

In 1979, the Daytona 500 became the first NASCAR stock car race that was nationally televised from beginning to end on the CBS television network. As the race's leaders went into the last lap of the race, drivers Cale Yarborough and Donnie Allison smashed their cars on the backstretch while fighting for the lead. This allowed driver Richard Petty to pass them both and win the race. Immediately, Yarborough, Allison, and Allison's brother Bobby got into a fistfight on national television.

The drama of the accident and then the fight caught the attention of viewers watching the events unfold on live television. It just so happened that the race coincided with a major snowstorm along the United States' Eastern seaboard. Stuck inside, millions of viewers who may have not seen this race otherwise were introduced to the wild and woolly world of NASCAR for the first time.

Year honors for his success in his first season in the Busch Series. He had won five races, secured four pole positions, had 15 top-five finishes, and 21 top-ten finishes. Edwards also finished third in the overall point standings.

Becoming a Fan Favorite

Edwards quickly began earning a reputation as a skilled driver. But he also became known for showing off his fun side, especially following race victories. Edwards became a fan favorite soon after he began doing backflips off of his car window to celebrate his victories. It all started when Edwards was about seven or eight years old. His mother, Nancy Sterling, remembers looking out the back window of her house just in time to see her son come down hard on the frame of a trampoline. That was the first time Sterling recalled seeing her son attempt a backflip. She didn't think much of it at the time, but Edwards worked hard to perfect the maneuver that would become his trademark.

The immediate inspiration for Edwards's post-race back-flips was Tyler Walker, a race car driver from California who also executed backflips after wins. Edwards decided the backflip might be a fun thing for him to try, too. His dad agreed. Edwards Sr. tipped off a photographer to his son's unusual post-victory ritual, and the photographer snapped a shot of the younger Edwards launching himself into a backflip. Soon, whenever Edwards won, everyone was cheering him on, waiting in anticipation to see him climb out of his car window, position himself on the door, and flip himself off of his car. Many fans began rooting for Edwards to win simply in the hopes of seeing his post-victory backflip.

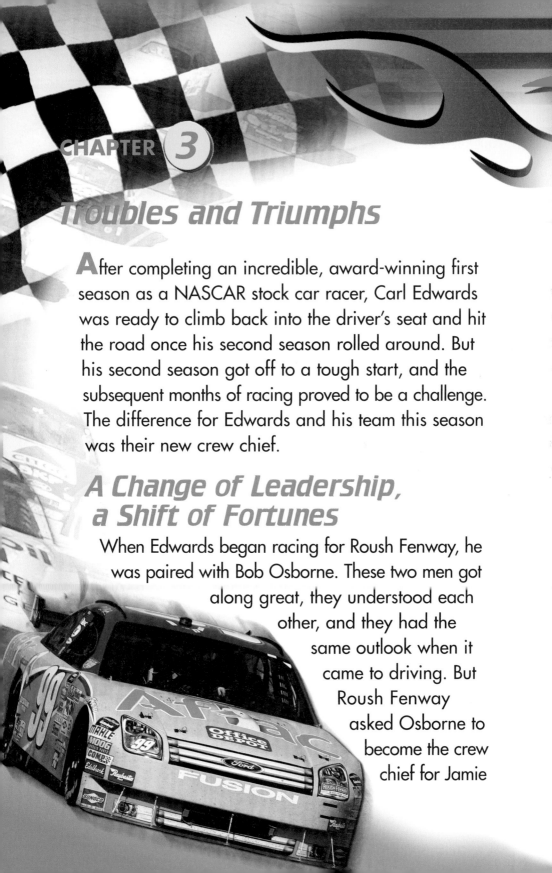

CHAPTER 3

Troubles and Triumphs

After completing an incredible, award-winning first season as a NASCAR stock car racer, Carl Edwards was ready to climb back into the driver's seat and hit the road once his second season rolled around. But his second season got off to a tough start, and the subsequent months of racing proved to be a challenge. The difference for Edwards and his team this season was their new crew chief.

A Change of Leadership, a Shift of Fortunes

When Edwards began racing for Roush Fenway, he was paired with Bob Osborne. These two men got along great, they understood each other, and they had the same outlook when it came to driving. But Roush Fenway asked Osborne to become the crew chief for Jamie

It takes an entire team to produce a win. Leading Edwards's team is Bob Osborne, his crew chief *(left)*. Osborne is in constant communication with Edwards and the pit crew during races.

McMurray, an up-and-coming driver who joined the Roush Fenway team in 2006. Edwards was now working with a new crew chief, and the outcome was drastically different.

In 2006, Edwards did not win a single race. His best finish all year was at the Michigan Speedway, where he finished in second place. Roush Fenway, seeing that the change in crew chief only hindered Edwards and failed to add to the momentum he built in his previous season, decided to move Osborne back to Edwards's team for the 2007 season. One thing that helped Edwards and Osborne get through the winless streak was strong communication. "We just have to be honest with each other, and we always are," Osborne said in an interview with *USA Today.* "Carl is a very intelligent person. He's constantly thinking about how he can be better on any given lap around the racetrack. He just has raw talent, and he's incredibly sharp. I think it's his intelligence that puts him ahead because he's constantly working on the next thing to make the car better."

The crew chief change, renewing his solid partnership with Osborne, helped Edwards break the 52-week winless streak on June 17, 2007. On that day, he won the Citizens Bank 400. Later that summer, on July 23, Edwards was

During each pit stop, within a matter of seconds, pit crews make sure tires are rotated or changed (depending on the track's condition), brake pads are replaced, and engine fluids are replenished.

slightly injured when he dislocated his thumb in an
11-car pileup at Nebraska Raceway Park. The injury
did little to slow him down. He won his second race of
the 2007 season—and sixth career Cup race—at the
Sharpie 500 at Bristol Motor Speedway on August 25.
During a post-race interview, Edwards talked about the
significance of the victory, calling it the biggest win of
his career.

At the conclusion of the first 26 races of the 2007
season, Edwards ranked sixth in overall standings. He
was only behind Jeff Gordon, one of NASCAR's best
and most popular drivers. Edwards continued to race
well through the remainder of the 2007 season. And
on November 3, he clinched his first NASCAR Busch
Series championship.

A Setback Stalls
a Promising Season

The 2008 season began with a bang for Edwards when
he won the 2008 Auto Club 500, his first Nextel Cup win
of the year. The following week, he won the UAW-Dodge
400 at Las Vegas Motor Speedway. These two wins marked
his first back-to-back victories since 2005. The wins also
put Edwards at the top of the point standings for the first
time in his career.

But there was little time to celebrate these victories.
Following the win in Las Vegas, NASCAR penalized

After winning the UAW-Dodge 400 at the Las Vegas Motor Speedway on March 2, 2008, a post-race inspection revealed that Edwards's car was in violation of several rules, resulting in a loss of points.

Edwards, Roush Fenway owner Jack Roush, and Edwards's crew chief, Bob Osborne, for violations found in a post-race inspection. After every race, cars are inspected to make sure they meet NASCAR criteria and rules. Edwards's #99 car was found to be in violation of several NASCAR rules. The most important of these infractions had been the removal of the cover from the car's oil tank. Due to these violations, Edwards was fined 100 points and stripped of the ten bonus points he had earned for the Las Vegas victory. Jack Roush was also fined 100 owner

UNDERSTANDING THE NASCAR POINTS SYSTEM

NASCAR holds races each week in the Sprint Cup Series, the Nationwide Series, and Craftsman Truck Series. Drivers work toward a year-end championship. But how do they determine who the champion is at the end of the year? It's all based on a points system.

Every race on the schedule is worth the same number of NASCAR points (except the Budweiser Shootout and the Sprint All-Star race, which are not worth any points at all). So, winning the famous Daytona 500 earns you the same number of points as winning a small race, like Watkins Glen. This makes each race of the season equally important.

Beginning with the 2007 season, NASCAR changed format for the points. Now, drivers compete in the Chase for the NASCAR Sprint Cup. Points are tallied after the first 26 races, and the top 12 drivers with the most points are locked into the Chase, which consists of the final ten races of the season. All 12 drivers have their points automatically set to 5,000, and ten points are added to each driver's score for every race won during the first 26 races of the season. During the final ten races, NASCAR points are still assigned the same way as

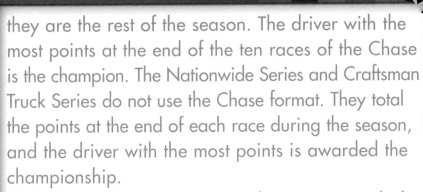

they are the rest of the season. The driver with the most points at the end of the ten races of the Chase is the champion. The Nationwide Series and Craftsman Truck Series do not use the Chase format. They total the points at the end of each race during the season, and the driver with the most points is awarded the championship.

Adding to the excitement are bonus points, which drivers earn for each lap they lead during a race. The driver who leads the most laps in each race is also awarded an additional five bonus points.

points, and Osborne was suspended for six races and fined $100,000.

Carl Edwards: A High-Performance Machine

Edwards quickly became known on the driving circuit as a relentless, super-competitive driver. He never backs down and fights for a lead position in every race. He has also become famous for his physique. *ESPN Magazine* named

Edwards has appeared on a number of magazine covers and has secured a number of product endorsements, including Claritin allergy medicine and Aflac insurance.

Edwards the "Most Ripped Driver in NASCAR" when he appeared on its cover. He is known to spend hours in the gym working out. For him, it's just one more necessary step toward properly preparing for a race.

In an interview with *Men's Fitness* magazine, Edwards talked about how fitness has become a large part of his winning strategy. "Driving is 90 percent mental," he said. "And the last 10 percent is where the physical side helps you. Just like someone who sits in an office all day, you're going to make better decisions if you're well-rested and in good physical shape."

Edwards's personal trainer, Dean Golich, created a workout program that keeps Edwards in great shape but also prepares him for the unique kind of exhaustion that can occur while racing. "When it's Sunday afternoon after he's raced two races already, and he needs to concentrate, and it's 140 degrees in the car, it's no problem for him," says Golich. Edwards told *Men's Fitness* that his workouts make him a better driver. "I simply don't feel like I ever get tired," he said. "I never feel bad. I can be driving in Mexico City, at 7,300 feet [2,225 meters], and I never feel tired. That can be huge when it's a hot, humid day."

This approach to driving is different and one that many other drivers are starting to embrace. According to Edwards, "I think NASCAR guys have realized in the last few years that if there's a way to get ahead, the gym is the best place to start."

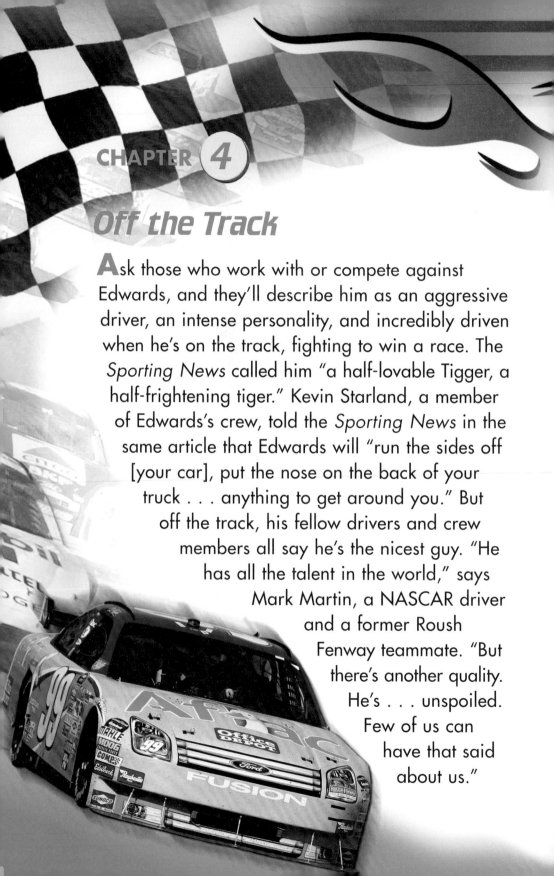

CHAPTER 4

Off the Track

Ask those who work with or compete against Edwards, and they'll describe him as an aggressive driver, an intense personality, and incredibly driven when he's on the track, fighting to win a race. The *Sporting News* called him "a half-lovable Tigger, a half-frightening tiger." Kevin Starland, a member of Edwards's crew, told the *Sporting News* in the same article that Edwards will "run the sides off [your car], put the nose on the back of your truck . . . anything to get around you." But off the track, his fellow drivers and crew members all say he's the nicest guy. "He has all the talent in the world," says Mark Martin, a NASCAR driver and a former Roush Fenway teammate. "But there's another quality. He's . . . unspoiled. Few of us can have that said about us."

Supporting the Local Music Scene

While Edwards lives in Mooresville, North Carolina, during the racing season, in the off-season he can be found in his hometown of Columbia, Missouri. Edwards's life away from the track centers around his friends and family. He's also active in music and children's charities. He has even found Hollywood calling.

Edwards loves music, so his brother and his friends would pass along songs recorded by some of Columbia's local bands. "I'd come home and my little brother and my buddies would give me these CDs that people were making, and they'd have to go to Kansas City or St. Louis to record stuff," he said in an interview with the *York Dispatch* newspaper. "It cost too much for them to do on a regular basis. And we all were just sitting there at the house, and we thought, why don't we just take this room of the house and make it a recording studio?" So, Edwards started a small record label, called Back40 Records, with Aaron Naeger, who also goes by the stage name Dex Hayes.

Edwards and Naeger met when they were both members of their high school marching band's drum line. The two friends established Back40 as an outlet for artists in Columbia to showcase their talent. "[The project] turned into a lot of fun," Edwards said in that same interview. The record company's name comes from his early days

As a music lover, Edwards, who plays guitar as a hobby, has established Back40 Records, a record label that is based in his hometown of Columbia, Missouri.

racing cars. "We'd have all these cars together and go race them out in this field that my buddy called his Back40 because it was his back 40 acres," Edwards said.

Making Young Fans' Dreams Come True

While his passion for music runs deep, Edwards's commitment to give back to his community runs even deeper. After giving up a career in education in favor of pursuing his dream of racing, Edwards became very involved in two major charitable organizations: the Dream Factory and the Victory Junction Gang.

The Dream Factory is an organization that seeks to grant the wishes of children diagnosed with critical or chronic illnesses. The children involved in the Dream Factory are between 3 and 18 years of age. Established in 1980, the Dream Factory has grown into the second-largest children's wish-granting organization in the United States. The organization has engineered opportunities for children to swim with dolphins, attend sporting events, and meet the president of the United States, celebrities, and athletes.

Not only does Edwards support the Dream Factory with financial contributions, he also has hosted meet-and-greet parties for kids and their families before races. He has invited children to watch NASCAR races with his pit crew and has introduced them to other drivers, too. Edwards even presented the trophy from his very first NASCAR win to Josh Bassinger, a Dream Factory participant from central Missouri. Giving away his trophies has become a sort of tradition for Edwards. "I give away my trophies because the most special things in life are the memories and experiences," he told *USA Today*. Edwards has given his trophies to children associated with the Dream Factory, as well as to family members and friends.

FUTURE HOME OF

VICTORY JUNCTION GANG.

OLE·IN·THE·WALL GANG CAMP

Edwards is heavily involved in the Victory Junction Gang, a race camp for children with serious illnesses. It was founded by NASCAR legend Kyle Petty *(above)* and his wife, Pattie.

Edwards has even found a way to combine his love of music with the Dream Factory. Back40 Records's first CD, entitled *That One CD*, is a mix of hip-hop, R&B, and rock music performed by seven different local artists. The album was released during a benefit concert in downtown Columbia. Edwards donated all of the proceeds from the concert to the Dream Factory Foundation.

Another organization Edwards supports is the Victory Junction Gang, founded by NASCAR legend Kyle Petty and his wife, Pattie. The Pettys created Victory Junction in honor of their son, Adam. Adam Petty had begun a promising career in racing but was killed in 2000 at the New Hampshire International Speedway following a practice run accident. The Pettys founded Victory Junction to give children with chronic medical conditions and serious illnesses the opportunity to have a camp experience that is exciting, fun, and empowering, and is conducted in a safe and medically sound environment.

Victory Junction is located in Randleman, North Carolina. The camp has a racing theme, providing the sights, sounds, look, and feel of a real racetrack. The grounds are composed of more than 44 buildings, including restaurants, a theater, a water park, and a race shop. The camp also has its own state-of-the-art medical center. This is what makes Victory Junction different from other types of camps. Victory Junction has the capacity to host sick children who would not otherwise be able to attend a camp because of their medical needs. The camp's medical staff includes doctors, nurses, and specialists to ensure that children receive their regular treatments and care while attending the camp.

Victory Junction is entirely funded by the donations of corporations, organizations, and individuals. The camp receives support from many NASCAR drivers, teams, and sponsors, including the telecommunications company Sprint, the Cup Series's primary sponsor.

Giving Back

Edwards has also become an Ambassador for Youth for the National PTA (Parent-Teacher Association). In this role, he helps to promote children's health and wellness. A fitness fanatic himself, Edwards knows the importance of physical and mental health. In a statement announcing his partnership with the National PTA, he said, "There is a lot of progress to be made to ensure that children are getting the right nutrients and vitamins while keeping a check on the bad things they eat and drink. I am excited to be part of such an important program and look forward to working hard to promote healthy lifestyles in children."

Edwards also uses his racing as a way to give back. He regularly participates in charitable races and donates a portion of his winnings to organizations in need. Edwards raced in the Prelude to the Dream at Eldora Speedway, a 30-lap charity race organized by fellow driver Tony

Edwards and teammate Tony Stewart, who both drive for the Roush Fenway Racing team, congratulate each other for a race well driven.

Stewart. More than 20,000 people attended the race, and HBO aired it as a pay-per-view special on television. All of the proceeds from the race went to the Tony Stewart Foundation and the Victory Junction Gang.

The Bright Lights of Hollywood

It doesn't take long once you've made it as a professional athlete for Hollywood to come calling. While Edwards was in California to promote a race at the California

EDWARDS'S WINNING DRIVING RECORD

Carl Edwards has logged a number of first place finishes in his brief but exciting career as a NASCAR driver. Here is a look at his wins:

Sprint Cup	2008	Samsung 500 (Texas Motor Speedway)
		Auto Club 500 (Auto Club Speedway)
		UAW-Dodge 400 (Las Vegas Motor Speedway)
	2007	Citizens Bank 400 (Michigan International Speedway)
		Sharpie 500 (Bristol Motor Speedway)
		Dodge Dealers 400 (Dover International Speedway)
	2005	Golden Corral 500 (Atlanta Motor Speedway)
		Pocono 500 (Pocono Raceway)
		Bass Pro Shops MBNA 500 (Atlanta Motor Speedway)
		Dickies 500 (Texas Motor Speedway)
Nationwide Series	2007	Sharpie Mini 300 (Bristol Motor Speedway)
		Pepsi 300 (Nashville Superspeedway)
		Dover 200 (Dover International Speedway)
		Federated Auto Parts 300 (Nashville Superspeedway)
	2006	Carquest Auto Parts 300 (Lowe's Motor Speedway)
		Federated Auto Parts 300 (Nashville Superspeedway)
		New England 200 (New Hampshire International Speedway)
		Busch Silver Celebration 250 (Gateway International Raceway)
	2005	Aaron's 312 (Atlanta Motor Speedway)
		Funai 250 (Richmond International Raceway)
		Meijer 300 presented by Oreo (Kentucky Speedway)
		Ameriquest 300 (California Speedway)
		Arizona 200 presented by Walk the Line (Phoenix International Raceway)
Craftsman Truck Series	2004	Florida Dodge Dealers 250 (Daytona International Speedway)
		O'Reilly Auto Parts 250 (Kansas Speedway)
		O'Reilly 200 presented by Valvoline Maxlife (Bristol Motor Speedway)
	2003	Built Ford Tough 225 (Kentucky Speedway)
		Power Stroke Diesel 200 (Indianapolis Raceway Park)

Speedway, he took time out to appear in an episode of the Fox Television Network's hit show *24*. On the show, Edwards played a Homeland Security agent named Jim Hill. In October 2005, he made a guest appearance as himself on the ABC soap opera *Guiding Light*.

When Electronic Arts, the video gaming company, contacted Edwards to see if he'd be interested in being featured in the 2007 edition of its NASCAR game, he became one of the few drivers who opted not to sign his name and likeness over to the company. Instead, Edwards lent his name to a series of plug-and-play video games made by Excalibur Electronics. This competing racing game even features Edwards's signature backflip, shown whenever his character wins a race. He has also endorsed a handheld LCD game, which is co-branded with NASCAR and is highlighted by red #99 Carl Edwards graphics.

Yet, no matter who or what may come calling for him as he wracks up race wins and gains even greater popularity—Hollywood directors, video game designers, product endorsements, the music industry, charitable projects—there is little doubt that Carl Edwards's main focus will remain his longtime passion: stock car racing. As he pursues his need for speed and victory with characteristic intensity, sportsmanship, and good humor, we can expect to see many more trademark celebratory backflips from the side of car #99.

Glossary

Craftsman Truck Series NASCAR's modified truck racing series. It was launched in 1995.

crew chief The head person on a pit stop. The crew chief's primary duties include developing car setups, configuring pit strategies, and receiving feedback from his driver about the car's handling. The crew chief has been compared to the head coach in other professional sports.

hot lapping Driving a vehicle on a racetrack without actually competing for a position.

modified stock cars Race cars that have been changed, or modified, from their original factory configuration. Modifying cars can enhance their performance.

NASCAR The National Association for Stock Car Auto Racing, the largest sanctioning body for stock car racing in the United States. NASCAR was founded in 1947.

Nationwide Series NASCAR's second-highest level of stock car racing. Nationwide cars are similar to, but less powerful than, the cars raced at NASCAR's top level. The Nationwide Series is named after its sponsor. In past years, it has been named the Busch Series (2004–2007), the Busch Grand National Series (1984–2003), and the Budweiser Late Model Sportsman Series (1982–1983).

owner points Owner points are distributed in the same manner as driver points, except that the owner receives points based on the performance of the car, regardless of who drives it. Owner points are used to determine the starting lineups when a qualifying race is canceled.

pit crew The members of the crew that work on a race car at the racetrack.

pit stop Also known as the pits, a pit stop is where a racing vehicle stops during a race for refueling, new tires, repairs, mechanical adjustments, a driver change, or any combination of the above.

pole position The number one starting position, usually earned by being the fastest driver during qualifying races.

Glossary

post-race inspection An inspection conducted after the race concludes to ensure the car meets the criteria set forth by NASCAR.

PTA Acronym for the Parent-Teacher Association, the largest volunteer child advocacy association in the nation.

qualifying laps Referring to the preliminary laps during which cars compete to earn a slot in a race. Cars race one at a time, as quickly as possible. Qualifying laps determine the order in which cars line up during the race.

sanctioning body An organization that sets and enforces rules and regulations for a certain type of racing.

spectator sport A sporting event that has a large audience that does not actively participate in the action but watches and cheers from the stands or in front of their television sets.

Sprint Cup NASCAR's top level of competition in which America's best stock car racers compete. The series is named after its sponsor, Sprint. It has also been called the Nextel Cup (2004–2007) and the Winston Cup (1972–2003).

stock car A race car with a body based on a street car that consumers can buy at regular dealerships.

For More Information

Grand American Road Racing Association
1801 West International Speedway Boulevard
Daytona Beach, FL 32114-1243
(386) 947-6681
Web site: http://www.grandamerican.com
The Grand American Road Racing Association was established in
1999 to return stability to major league sports car road racing in
North America.

The NASCAR Foundation
One Wachovia Center
301 South College Street, Suite 3900
Charlotte, NC 28202
Web site: http://foundation.nascar.com
The NASCAR Foundation supports a wide range of charitable initiatives
that reflect the core values of the entire NASCAR family. The
foundation uses the strength of the sport and its people to make
a difference in the lives of those who need it most.

National Association for Stock Car Auto Racing, Inc. (NASCAR)
P.O. Box 2875
Daytona Beach, FL 32120
(386) 253-0611
Web site: http://www.nascar.com
NASCAR is the sanctioning body for stock car and truck racing.

Roush Fenway Racing Museum
4600 Roush Place NW
Concord, NC 28027
Web site: http://www.roushfenwaycorporate.com/Museum/default.asp
This museum, created by Roush Fenway Racing, one of the leading
NASCAR racing teams, includes historic race cars from the drag

racing past up to the NASCAR present. It also includes a theater and interactive displays.

Web Sites

Due to the changing nature of Internet links, Rosen Publishing has developed an online list of Web sites related to the subject of this book. This site is updated regularly. Please use this link to access this list:

http://www.rosenlinks.com/bw/caed

For Further Reading

Buckley, James, Jr. *NASCAR*. New York, NY: Dorling Kindersley Children, 2005.

Burt, William. *NASCAR's Best: Top Drivers Past and Present*. Osceola, WI: Motorbooks, 2004.

Fielden, Greg. *NASCAR: The Complete History*. New York, NY: Publications International, 2007.

Leslie-Pelecky, Diandra. *The Physics of NASCAR: How to Make Steel + Gas + Rubber = Speed*. New York, NY: Dutton Adult, 2008.

McLaurin, Jim. *Then Junior Said to Jeff: The Best NASCAR Stories Ever Told*. Chicago, IL: Triumph Books, 2006.

Schaefer, A. R. *The History of NASCAR*. Mankato, MN: Capstone Press, 2005.

Stevens, Josh, and Matthew Heidenry. *Carl Edwards* (The Reedy Series). St. Louis, MO: Reedy Press, 2006.

Yates, Brock. *NASCAR Off the Record*. Osceola, WI: Motorbooks, 2004.

Bibliography

Dallenbach, Robin, and Anita Rich. *Portraits of NASCAR*. Marietta, GA: Motorsports Family LLC, 2008.

Gunn, Jon. "Mixin' It Up with Carl Edwards." SceneDaily.com, October 1, 2007. Retrieved April 26, 2008 (http://www.scenedaily.com/lifestyle/How_Carl_Edwards_Helps_Musicians_Fulfill_Their_Dreams.html).

Krone, Nikki. "Carl Edwards to Compete for the Ultimate Father's Day Gift—Back-to-Back NEXTEL Cup Victories." FrontStretch.com, June 17, 2005. Retrieved April 18, 2008 (http://www.frontstretch.com/nkrone/552).

Newton, David. "Edwards Gets High Marks for His Post-Victory Backflip." ESPN.com, March 7, 2008. Retrieved April 26, 2008 (http://sports.espn.go.com/rpm/columns/story?columnist=newton_david&id=3281268).

O'Connor, Brian. "Fittest Man in NASCAR." *Men's Fitness*. Retrieved April 22, 2008 (http://www.mensfitness.com/carl_edwards/exclusives/169).

PR.com. "Carl Edwards Celebrating CD Release with a Benefit Concert." January 24, 2007. Retrieved April 25, 2008 (http://www.pr.com/press-release/27910).

PTA.org. "NASCAR Driver Named Ambassador for Youth to Promote Children's Health and Wellness." April 10, 2006. Retrieved May 1, 2008 (http://www.pta.org/ne_press_release_detail_1144684031546.html).

Siska, Ellen. "NASCAR Driver Carl Edwards Stays in Tune Off the Track." *York Dispatch*, December 11, 2006. Retrieved April 18, 2008 (http://yorkdispatch.inyork.com/sports/ci_4818530).

Turner, Jared. "Roush Says Edwards Communicates Well with Team Engineers." SceneDaily.com, April 8, 2008. Retrieved April 18, 2008 (http://www.scenedaily.com/news/articles/sprintcupseries/Roush_says_Edwards_communicates_well_with_team_engineers.html).

Index

B

Back40 Records, 33–35, 40

D

Dream Factory, 35–37

E

Edwards, Carl, Jr.
  awards/honors, 4, 9, 13, 18,
    19, 20–21, 26
  backflips and, 22
  early life of, 6–13
  education and, 13, 35
  fitness and, 31, 38
  injury and, 26
  music and, 33–35
  penalties and, 26–27
  television and, 41
  video games and, 41
Edwards, Carl, Sr., 6, 9, 22

I

International Motor Contest
    Association (IMCA), 12–13

J

Johnson, Jimmie, 20

K

Kenseth, Matt, 19

L

Labonte, Terry, 19

M

Martin, Mark, 17, 32
Mittler, Mike, 14, 16

N

NASCAR
  Busch Series, 4–5, 16, 19, 20, 26
  Craftsman Truck Series, 4, 14,
    16, 18, 19, 20, 28, 29
  history of, 14–16
  Hornet Division, 7
  Nationwide Series, 15, 16, 19,
    28, 29
  Nextel Cup Series, 15, 18,
    20, 26
  points system of, 28–29
  Sprint Cup Series, 15, 16,
    18–19, 28, 38
  Winston Cup Series, 15

O

Osborne, Bob, 23, 24–25, 27, 29

P

Petty, Kyle, 19, 37

R

Roush Fenway Racing, 17, 19,
    23, 24, 27, 32

V

Victory Junction Gang, 35,
    37–38, 39

CARL EDWARDS:

About the Author

Laura La Bella is a writer and editor who lives in Rochester, New York. She is an avid sports fan who loves baseball (New York Yankees) and hockey (Buffalo Sabres). She grew up watching NASCAR races with her father, a devoted fan. This is La Bella's fourth biography for Rosen Publishing.

Photo Credits

Designer: Evelyn Horovicz; Photo Researcher: Cindy Reiman